I0410916

TABLE OF CONTENTS

ACRONYMS

ARCENT	United States Army Central (Third Army)
CENTCOM	United States Central Command
CIS	Commonwealth of Independent States
CNPC	China National Petroleum Corporation
CSTO	Combined Security Treaty Organization
IMU	I Islamic Movement of Uzbekistan
KMG	KazMunaiGaz, Kazakhstan's national oil company
OPEC	Organization of the Petroleum Exporting Countries
SCO	Shanghai Cooperation Organization, originally known as the "Shanghai 5"
USTRANSCOM	United States Transportation Command
USSR	Union of Soviet Socialist Republics

TABLES

INTRODUCTION

> US engagement in Central Asia is no longer a given. It's not something we can take for granted, nor is it something that is necessarily desired by the states of Central Asia—specifically, by the leadership of these countries.
>
> —Roger Kangas[1]

Central Asia consists of five former-Soviet republics: Kazakhstan, Kyrgyzstan, Tajikistan, Turkmenistan, and Uzbekistan. These five states encompass a vast expanse of territory, generally sparsely populated with pockets of higher density according to the arability of the land. The region is landlocked, isolated from any seaport, yet rich in mineral and energy wealth. Despite traditional ties to the Russian Federation from its days as part of the Union of Soviet Socialist Republics (USSR), as well as its nations' proximity to one of the world's most rapidly expanding economies in China, the Central Asian states have managed to maintain their freedom of action and overall autonomy. Central Asia's governments, despite their authoritarian overtones, have typically led their respective countries capably since independence, despite, or perhaps because of, numerous pressures from outside influences. How have these Central Asian regimes managed this balancing of influences from the major powers of Russia, China, and the United States, as well as internal influences within Central Asia? How should the actions of Central Asia's governments in accordance with their own self-interest inform and influence United States' theater security cooperation and military-to-military engagements? This monograph seeks to answer these questions, so that operational planners might benefit from a better understanding of where cooperation with the United States fits in the Central Asian states' collective worldview.

---

[1]Joshua Kucera, "Central Asia: Washington Must Adapt to Diminished Role in Central Asia," Eurasianet.org, http://www.eurasianet.org/node/66253 (accessed March 20, 2013). Dr. Roger Kangas, professor of Central Asian Studies at the National Defense University, is quoted in this article, but no citation is attributed by the author.

Organization

Included in this monograph are five main body sections that highlight the Central Asian states' actions in their self-interest by balancing the effects of the major actors who seek to influence it. The introduction of this monograph provides the primary research question, background on Central Asia's importance, and the operational and intellectual impetus for the monograph. The Literature Review presents overarching international relations theories and models that are helpful to understanding the actions of all parties involved, as well as a more detailed view of how the major powers view their interactions with each other and Central Asia. Finally, the review provides an analysis that ties actions and models together to provide a coherent understanding of interactions between the major powers that affect Central Asia, and their interactions with Central Asian nations.

The case study section provides a methodology for case selection, structure, and evaluation. The two case studies on military engagement and energy highlight Kazakhstan's actions over the last two decades and provide a point of reference to apply international relations theory to aid in determining future courses of action. A third case study, which looks at United States' regional basing, sheds further light on how balancing occurs in Central Asia. The analysis section integrates the findings of the three case studies within the framework of international relations theory, in order to promote understanding of the Central Asian states' past actions and provide context for future actions. The conclusion recommends a method of thinking for operational planners working on exercises and theater security cooperation in Central Asia, and proposes further research on other applicable international relations theories.

Background

Communism finally fell in Central Asia in 1991. However, the local communist party ruling elites remained in power, ruling independent states instead of mere portions of a union.[2] The ruling elites who came to power under the Soviet system have maintained power since independence. While the region has an abundance of natural resources and is important as a crossroad of interaction between Russia and China, the United States and Europe largely ignored Central Asia for over a decade.

Following the attacks on September 11, 2001, the world began to recognize Central Asia's strategic importance. The region's population was mostly Muslim, but predominately a more moderate form than elsewhere in the Islamic world due to the former influence of Soviet control. Central Asia was able to avoid much of the extremism to its south, but a rising Islamic identity in the region did produce pockets of radicalism. This fact, as well as its ties to Russia and location near the then-recognized Al Qaida stronghold in Afghanistan, increased status of the region in the eyes of the United States, as well as the remainder of the NATO nations.

Operational and Intellectual Relevance

Many have said that the world changed significantly following the terrorist attacks on September 11, 2001. While the world itself did not suddenly change, the United States' perspective of it did. United States' foreign policy had largely overlooked Central Asia up to this point. However, with war looming in Afghanistan, Central Asia took on new meaning to provide initial access and logistics sustainment to Operation Enduring Freedom.

---

[2]Alexander Cooley, *Great Games, Local Rules: The New Great Power Contest in Central Asia* (New York: Oxford University Press, 2012), 16, Kindle e-book.

NATO Operation Steppe Eagle, held annually since 2006, has been one of the cornerstones of NATO's assistance to Kazakhstan.[3] Held in the early fall at the Ilisky Training Center, it typically involves British forces as trainers and opposing force, with the United States bringing exercise simulation support and providing a notional NATO division headquarters for the Kazakh brigade. Kazakhstan specifically designed the brigade in question (KAZBRIG) to operate as part of a multi-national force, typically noted as either operating with the United Nations or NATO, but fully capable of operating within any of the other security cooperation agreements that Kazakhstan has made with its neighbors. However, as of 2010, the KAZBRIG was at approximately 50% strength, with one full-strength, well-trained battalion (KAZBAT), one severely under-strength battalion with little training, and one battalion which existed only on paper.[4] *It was the author's participation in two consecutive iterations of this exercise, and the perception among the United States Army Central (ARCENT) staff involved that Kazakhstan was not allocating full resources to a major training event with the United States, but instead dividing its resources between that event and one with China later in the year, that ultimately prompted the questioning behind this monograph.*

Due to its large geographic area, significant raw material resources, and relatively stable governments, Central Asia plays a large role in the region's stability and prosperity. Major nations, such as China, Russia, and the United States, attempt to influence the Central Asian governments to varying degrees, both to obtain some good directly for themselves, as well as to use those governments as part of an overall policy for Central Asia. The individual self-interests

---

[3]North Atlantic Treaty Organization, "NATO's Relations with Kazakhstan," North Atlantic Treaty Organization, http://www.nato.int/cps/en/natolive/topics_49598.htm (accessed September 27, 2012).

[4]Author's personal observations as part of the ARCENT exercise staff for OPERATION Steppe Eagle 2010.

of the Central Asian states work both with, and occasionally against, the interests of the major powers. This confluence of interests requires further examination to understand, in order to avoid unintended effects between the United States and Central Asian interests, specifically military cooperation interests.

LITERATURE REVIEW

Why International Relations Theory?

Theories of interaction between groups generally acknowledge a higher set of rules above those of the group itself. Business theories must follow the rule of law in the countries where the businesses in question operate. The same holds true for management theories. Both of these could be somewhat applicable to viewing the relations between sovereign states, but both still assume a higher set of rules and laws. However, at its basis, international relations theory assumes a state of anarchy in the interactions between states.[5] Unlike interactions between groups within a state, which have as a higher system the government and laws of that state itself, there is no world government to control the actions of the various states.

Prior to the breakup of the USSR, the Central Asian states were part of the Soviet state.[6] However, with the breakup of the Soviet Union in late 1991, the Central Asian Republics emerged as independent states, bringing them out from under the higher system umbrella of the Soviet Union and into the anarchy that is part of being a sovereign state in our current world. The point at which the republics became states thus becomes the starting point for applying international relations theory to them.

---

[5]Stephen M. Walt, "International Relations: One World, Many Theories," *Foreign Policy* no. 110 (Spring 1998), 31, http://www.jstor.org/stable/10.2307/1149275 (accessed September 28, 2012).

[6]Robert Legvold, ed., *Thinking Strategically: the Major Powers, Kazakhstan, and the Central Asian Nexus* (Cambridge: MIT Press, 2003), 17.

Multiple international relations theories abound to try to explain the actions of international actors, both state and non-state. These theories all have separate ways of looking at how states and other groups interact. Each has value in helping to give broader meaning to Kazakhstan's actions in dealing with the major powers, as well as its Central Asian neighbors and other states, in its conduct of international relations. Of these theories, realism and liberal institutionalism are the two overarching international relations lenses that best highlight how the Central Asian states conduct their foreign policy, and allow further analysis of these governments' actions.

Realism looks at states in a struggle for power, with the basic interactions between states conducted in a state of anarchy.[7] Anarchy, in this sense, is a lack of higher control, instead of its typical definition as unconstrained nihilism for its own sake. In international relations, there is no higher authority than the individual states themselves, and thus no overarching constraints on their actions, except where their neighbors react to their actions. At its core, it hearkens back to the Melian Dialogue: "the strong do what they have the power to do and the weak accept what they have to accept."[8]

While realism focuses on the actions of states as actors unto themselves, liberal institutionalism takes into account the fact that a confluence of interests often produces the formation of an alliance or other structure to further those interests.[9] Member states build institutions to address a common interest. Conversely, institutions thus serve the interests of their

---

[7]Walt, "International Relations," 31.

[8]*The Landmark Thucydides: A Comprehensive Guide to the Peloponnesian War*, ed. Robert Strassler (New York: Free Press, 1998), 349-357.

[9]Jack Snyder, "One World, Rival Theories," Foreign Policy, http://www.foreignpolicy.com/articles/2004/11/01/one_world_rival_theories (accessed April 2, 2013).

member states. The interests represented by the institution are important, but are not necessarily the various members' overall best interests. In gaining collectively, the individual states cede some of their less important interests and part of their sovereignty to ensure that the institution at large meets their major needs. Adopting this view of international relations is useful when states are willing to compromise with respect to their sovereignty, but is less relevant when states are unwilling to cede any of their sovereignty to a multilateral organization.

The basis for understanding how states interact in a realist system is balance of power theory. Kenneth Waltz looks at this theory in light of the period immediately following the Cold War, when some international relations scholars thought that realism was no longer useful as a lens to view nation-state interactions throughout the world.[10] Some viewed liberalism as the newly preferred lens, especially given the wave of nominal democratization that swept the former Soviet Union. However, as Waltz points out, the international system is still anarchy, with each member looking out for its own interests, yet colluding with others when those interests overlap sufficiently to overcome mistrust.

Waltz' greatest criticism of liberal institutionalism is that powerful states create organizations only for their own ends. If this is true, there will be structures that look like liberal institutions within Central Asia and encompassing one or more of the major powers.[11] However, these will be an epiphenomenon, where the interactions within these structures will be largely bilateral, with the smaller members interacting directly with the major power, as opposed to the truly multilateral relationships that liberal institutionalism predicts. The institutional structure

---

[10]Waltz, "Structural Realism after the Cold War," in *America Unrivaled: the Future of the Balance of Power*, ed. G. John Ikenberry (Ithaca: Cornell University Press, 2002), 29.

[11]Waltz, *America Unrivaled*, 42.

exists largely because it is a norm within the international community for it to exist, not because it serves a multilateral purpose.

When Waltz' views on institutions are applied to Central Asia, one should see institutional structures that encompass one or more of the major powers, as well as the majority of the Central Asian states, regardless of whether their interactions are realist or liberal institutionalist. If they follow Waltz's realist construct, the majority of interstate actions will be between one of the Central Asian states and one of the major powers, emphasizing both the interests of the major power and the single minor power over the interest of the collective group. However, if they follow Walt's concepts of liberal institutionalism, the interactions will involve multilateral agreements among all states in the institutional structure aimed at a common interest.[12]

Balance of Threat is a necessary offshoot of Balance of Power theory, as overall Balance of Power fails to explain the low level to which the remainder of the world has balanced against United States' presumed unipolarity.[13] Stephen Walt proposes four factors that help to understand how states choose to balance based on threats. The first factor is overall relative power, which in the case of any of the three major powers respective to Central Asian nations is quite unequal. Second, proximity of the two states lends stature to the ability to use overall power. In this, the United States, being much further from Central Asia than either Russia or China, receives a lower threat judgment than its power would suggest. Third, the offensive power of a nation, not just its overall power, lends credence to any threat it might make. Finally, the offensive intentions of a nation provide the final decision as to what constitutes a threat.

---

[12]Walt, "International Relations," 38.

[13]Stephen M. Walt, "Keeping the World "Off-Balance": Self-Restraint and U.S. Foreign Policy," in *America Unrivaled: The Future of the Balance of Power*, ed. G. John Ikenberry (Ithaca: Cornell University Press, 2002), 133-134.

The interaction of the three major powers with the Central Asian states provides the smaller states multiple opportunities to balance threats, based on their individual interpretations of Walt's four factors.[14] If these states operate according to realism, then they will tend to balance threats to their national sovereignty by bandwagoning with another major power. When one of the major powers introduces demands that a smaller state finds threatening, there are two other major powers available to bandwagon with to offset the threat. Bandwagoning can occur three ways. First, the smaller state might bandwagon with the major power that it sees as least threatening. Second, the smaller state might bandwagon with the major power that both helps to protect it from threat and gives it the greatest gain. Third, it may bandwagon with both of the non-threatening major powers. This third bandwagoning method can be problematic, as the interests of the major powers can lead to conflicts between the two, with the smaller state caught in the middle.

However, if the smaller states operate according to liberal institutionalism, they will find a common interest in balancing against a threatening major power. This common interest will limit bandwagoning, and instead bring about multilateral cooperation to deal with the threat. Rather than working with one of the other two major powers to counteract a threat from one major power, the Central Asian states will instead band together to pool their power and resources to mitigate the threat, without turning to more powerful influencers for assistance.

A final aspect of both overall realism and the realist interactions of balance of threat is that actions between parties will generally be a quid pro quo exchange, with both states acting in their self-interest and gaining something from the partnership. If the Central Asian states are operating according to realism, they will work with the major powers, but only if it benefits both

---

[14]Walt, *America Unrivaled*, 134-140.

them and the major power in question. These interactions will be largely bilateral, with neither side giving up a portion of its sovereignty to get what it wants.

However, if the Central Asian states operate according to liberal intuitionalism, the interaction between the parties will be multilateral instead of bilateral. The states will band together for a common interest, with all states benefitting from the multilateral interaction. As in any multilateral system, however, not all states will benefit equally. They will also tend to cede some of their sovereignty to the institution in order to allow the institution to function, trading that amount of sovereignty for collective benefit with their multilateral partners.

While international relations theory is important to understanding the interactions between the five Central Asian states and the three major powers, it is only the foundation for understanding what is important in the region. International relations theory helps to distinguish how the various regimes think about the various issues important to them. A more in-depth review of just over two decades worth of Central Asian international relations literature is necessary to determine what issues are important to the Central Asian states and the major powers, and to see how the various authors capture issues according to international relations theory.

Central Asia: International Relations Literature

While literature on Central Asia looks as far back as prehistoric culture, the literature written since the fall of the Soviet Union is the only literature capable of viewing the Central Asian states as what they are today: independent states. While literature pertaining to the period prior to the dissolution of the Soviet Union is useful in understanding how these states came into being, and how the initial conditions for their interactions were set, this literature is largely beyond the scope of this monograph.

One book to discuss Central Asian international relations following the fall of communism and the breakup of the Soviet Union in 1991 was Zbigniew Brzezinski's 1997 *The*

Grand Chessboard: American Primacy and Its Geostrategic Imperatives. Central Asia was not, however, the primary focus of this book, but merely an ancillary piece of Brzezinski's larger focus on Eurasia as a whole. Brzezinski saw Eurasia as critical to United States' foreign policy for a large number of reasons, including the emerging European Union, the former Soviet states and Soviet-influenced states, an emerging China, and a powerful Japan.[15] In short, it controlled most of the world's wealth and capacity for economic growth. Throughout Brzezinski's work, he argued for a comprehensive, integrated United States' international relations strategy for Eurasia as a whole.

Brzezinski's main argument was that the United States could not deal effectively with any one portion of Eurasia without an effective foreign policy that dealt with the whole of Eurasia, not just its individual pieces. In making his argument, he broke Eurasia down into component parts, analyzed these parts, and then synthesized them back into an entire system. Only once his reader understood each piece of the system could they understand how the pieces were connected and how the system as a whole functioned. Brzezinski's system in Central Asia included the security interests stemming from ethnic and religious tension, the fact that economics could ameliorate some of these security interests, and the energy infrastructure of the oil pipelines.

Brzezinski's work has two major problems, in light of this monograph's focus on Central Asia. First, his approach is extremely top-down, driven by the realist desires of the United States in its role of the sole remaining superpower. Despite the fact that he views Eurasia as an interconnected entity, he largely dismisses the ability of smaller states to balance the power of larger ones. Brzezinski's bias is readily apparent in his title *The Grand Chessboard*, with the

---

[15]Zbigniew Brzezinski, *The Grand Chessboard: American Primacy and Its Geostrategic Imperatives* (New York: Basic Books, 1997), chap. 2, under "The Eurasian Chessboard," Kindle e-book.

United States and other major powers as the chess masters. The second is his seeming dismissal of China's role in Central Asia. While he felt that China would seek energy security from this region, he structured his book in such a way that he failed to look for further linkages between the two.

In all, Brzezinski argued from a decidedly realist point of view in the portions of his work on Central Asia. Most of his views regarding the interaction between the United States, Russia, China, and the then-new Central Asian states stressed the fact that each entity will act in its own self-interest, despite the fact that self-interest may cause conflict with other states. He addressed liberalism only in passing, despite organizations like the Commonwealth of Independent States that had already formed, and the possibility that other institutions would further enmesh Central Asia and the major players.

Despite the realist strength of Brzezinski's views, the Russians are even more staunchly realist, albeit with a slightly less top-down view into Central Asia. Both Vitaly Naumkin and Lena Jonson examined Russian foreign policy in Central Asia.[16] Their focus areas were different, with Naumkin focusing primarily on Kazakhstan and Jonson excluding it, but their overall arguments were similar. Their general thesis was that the Russians needed to develop better policies with respect to Central Asia, which would allow them to project power more effectively on the international stage. This thesis also recognized that the policies the Russians followed up to the early 2000s linked to disjointed strategies and often antagonized those whom the Russians were attempting to influence.

---

[16]Lena Jonson, *Vladimir Putin and Central Asia: The Shaping of Russian Foreign Policy*, (London: I. B. Tauris, 2004), 13; Vitaly Naumkin, "Russian Policy Toward Kazakhstan," in *Thinking Strategically: the Major Powers, Kazakhstan, and the Central Asian Nexus*, ed. Robert Legvold, (Cambridge: MIT Press, 2003), 39-41.

Their main arguments revolved around Russia's central interests in Central Asia. These were relatively straightforward during the first ten years of independence, encompassing energy, the Russian diaspora, Russia's southern security buffer zone, and Moscow's historic sphere of influence. While Russian policy toward Central Asia may seem static at first glance, it has evolved slowly both in terms of its aims and the ways in which it attempts to get there. Naumkin views the first five years after independence as nothing but sheer pragmatism, very much in line with the "consequentialist" label that Ryan Lizza applied to many of President Obama's policies.[17] This largely stems from the complex, unfamiliar situation that the Russians found themselves in following the breakup of the USSR, in which they had to take small steps to test the reaction of the new international system, in order to develop more coherent long-term strategies.

As Lena Jonson points out, Russian policy toward Central Asia evolved in fits and starts based on opportunities presented within the international community, particularly centered on the Al Qaida attacks on the United States in 2001. This turning point in the international community allowed Russia to align its security strategy toward the former republics using anti-terrorism as the vehicle. The republics had dealt with separatist and dissident groups both within and crossing their respective borders for years. The September 11 attacks focused international attention on the problem, and opened security cooperation inroads for all three major powers within Central Asia. The United States and Russia moved first through military-based security cooperation, while China largely continued unchanged from its original course of undercutting dissident groups through economic prosperity.

Both of these lines followed realist thinking, both for the major powers employing them to gain increased access and influence in Central Asia, and for the Central Asian states who also

---

[17]Ryan Lizza, "The Consequentialist: How the Arab Spring Remade Obama's Foreign Policy," The New Yorker, http://www.newyorker.com/reporting/2011/05/02/110502fa_fact_lizza (accessed November 18, 2012).

benefitted by increased regime stability through increased help in dealing with terrorist groups. Much of the increased stability, however, was not due solely to anti-terror operations, but also operations against separatist and dissident groups that the Central Asian leaders lumped together under the taxonomy of terrorism. This stability promotion shows realist tendencies on the part of Central Asian leaders, who quite rationally choose to take actions necessary to protect their power.

Just as Russia's interaction with Central Asia progressed since independence, so too has the United States' thinking moved forward on how to deal with Central Asia. Robert Legvold's writing makes clear that, while the United States lost much of its interest in Central Asia between the end of the Soviet Union's war in Afghanistan and the beginning of United States' involvement there, it was quick to realize that the instability in Afghanistan might spread to the remainder of Central Asia.[18] This realization ties directly to his thesis that Central Asia, despite its landlocked nature and seeming unimportance, is actually a vital connection point within Asia and worth the United States' expenditure of effort to maintain influence in the region.

Legvold argues a number of ideas on the direction that United States' policy should take. The United States needs to recognize interdependence of the Central Asian states and create policies that take the overall inter-state system into account, rather than dealing with one piece of that system at a time.[19] Likewise, the United States needs to make sure no one major power gains dominance within Central Asia, in order to keep Central Asia as a meeting place, rather than a buffer for either Russia or China. Finally, the United States needs to focus not on control, but on a negative aim of avoiding instability. In doing this, the United States needs to avoid engaging in another long-term large-scale intervention as in Afghanistan, and instead head off small-scale

_____

[18]Legvold, 2-3.

[19]Ibid., 105.

14

problems early. He feels the United States needs to take a greater role within the region, although one where the elements of national power are in better alignment, rather than the military-dominant engagement he saw in 2003 and which is still visible today. He also sees a greater role for other institutions in Central Asia, especially the European Union.

Despite renewed US interest in Central Asia, Legvold's writing indicates that the United States still had a myopic overall vision of the Central Asian states as pawns on Brzezinski's chessboard. The first ten years of Soviet-based policies that tended to lump the Central Asian states together as a group without recognizing their individual contexts had not yet dissolved. Partly, though, this grouping is true, as the former Soviet policies inextricably linked the former republics for a number of years. However, they also each jealously guard their individual sovereignty, which tends to push policy toward multiple bilateral agreements instead of one multilateral one.

Despite United States authors' shift toward trying to understand what the Central Asian states want instead of merely looking at what the United States wants, the Kazakh authors within *Thinking Strategically* give little insight into what Kazakhstan actually views as being in its own best interest. Sultanov and Muzaparova do lay out the five underlying ends that Kazakhstan has attempted to pursue through balanced relations with the major powers, just not the why behind it. Kazakhstan had conducted its international relations balancing act to equalize influence of external actors, attract foreign investment, normalize the international environment, strengthen its independence, and guarantee its external security.[20] Even without knowing exactly why these aims have been chosen, it is apparent that all of them fall within a realist school of thought, as none of them overtly seek to push Kazakh ideals on their neighbors, nor to engage those

---

[20]Bulat Sultanov and Leila Muzaparova, "Great Power Policies and Interests in Kazakhstan," in *Thinking Strategically: the Major Powers, Kazakhstan, and the Central Asian Nexus*, ed. Robert Legvold (Cambridge: MIT Press, 2003), 188.

neighbors in institutions without balancing institutional ties among all three major powers. With these stated aims as a basis for understanding, the case studies coupled with later authors' arguments about why Kazakhstan pursues these aims will give a better context for understanding Kazakh motives for action.

While the United States and Russia have both traditionally viewed Central Asia from an external perspective, China has from the very beginning sought to understand the complex context of the region and pursue policies commensurate with it. Xing Guangcheng's 2003 writing identifies two key Chinese foreign policy priorities: great power diplomacy focused on Russia and the United States, and surrounding border diplomacy based on proximity to China.[21] His thesis is that within Central Asia both priorities overlap, with Russia attempting to maintain its traditional influence, the United States expanding its influence to support its Afghanistan efforts and limit further regional instability, and China's concern for its own border regions. As a result, China will expend increased effort

Both Guangcheng and Hassan Karrar identify the security and stability of Xinjiang province as being China's overarching concern. This province has always been at the outer limits of Chinese authority, and has a number of underlying social, economic, and ethnic rifts. The primary Chinese strategy for ameliorating these is economic development for Xinjiang province.[22] In order to make this development a reality, trade with Central Asia is a necessary factor that benefits both China and the Central Asian states. Energy, as well, helps cement the

---

[21]Xing Guangcheng, "China's Foreign Policy Toward Kazakhstan," in *Thinking Strategically: The Major Powers, Kazakhstan, and the Central Asian Nexus*, ed. Robert Legvold (Cambridge: MIT Press, 2003), 107.

[22]Guangcheng, 120-125; Hasan H. Karrar, *The New Silk Road Diplomacy: China's Central Asian Foreign Policy Since the Cold War* (Vancouver: UBC Press, 2010), 78.

relationships across this space with pipeline construction tying the various regions together, as well as serving China's energy security.

The way Guangcheng and Karrar view trade between China and the Central Asian states it borders falls squarely within the realm of realism, as the agreements are bilateral, not multilateral.[23] In this way, the Central Asian states fully preserve their sovereignty, and both sides benefit from the agreement. The same is largely true in the energy sector. However, the fact that the pipelines to China stretch beyond Kazakhstan into Russia ensures that some level of multilateral cooperation on energy must take place. Further cooperation will be necessary if the pipeline consortium makes the proposed extensions to Iran, Azerbaijan, or eventually all the way through Afghanistan and Pakistan to India.

One thing that both China experts largely ignored is the increasing military cooperation as part of the Shanghai Cooperation Organization (SCO). In the last decade, the SCO has served as the umbrella organization for nine bilateral and multilateral military exercises, involving Russia, China, and the Central Asian states.[24] While this military cooperation is small compared to economics and energy, it has the potential to grow in scale and deserves further examination.

While the Chinese have recognized from the beginning that bilateral engagements, which benefit both parties and avoid challenges to either party's sovereignty are extremely useful, the United States has taken a number of years to move in this direction. Michael D. Mihalka's 2007 article, "Not Much of a Game: Security Dynamics in Central Asia," is the first true United States' departure from looking at Central Asia solely in terms of what the major power wants, and begins to more strongly integrate how the interests of the Central Asian states trump our own in their

---

[23]Guangcheng, 127-128; Karrar, 156-157.

[24]PLA Daily, "The 9 Joint Military Exercises under SCO Framework," PLA Daily of the Chinese People's Liberation Army, http://eng.chinamil.com.cn/special-reports/2012-06/12/content_4892903.htm (accessed March 18, 2013).

backyard. He focuses on three reasons for United States' interest in the region: oil, terrorism, and Central Asia as "an arena for geopolitical and ideological competition."[25] His thesis is that, after analyzing these three reasons, the United States has no stake beyond maintaining the 2007 status quo in the region, and should not invest increased time or resources, as they would achieve little gain.

Mihalka's main arguments focus on proving this thesis. In terms of energy, Central Asia is distinctly disadvantageous to the United States because it sends all of its oil and natural gas either through Russia to the European Union and other European customers, or east into China. From a security standpoint, following the defeat of Al Qaida and the Taliban in Afghanistan, radical Islam has found no base of support in Central Asia, leaving us little to use as leverage in that area. Finally, in a purely international relations focus, Central Asia is one place where the ideologies and policies of the three major players most directly come in contact and competition, and should be used as a forum for the three major powers to interact, outside of other direct interaction on the world stage. All of these come from pure realism, with little trace of any multilateralism and its attendant widely shared goals. However, they do share some liberal institutionalist tones, as Mihalka promotes a shift from a unilaterally United States led policy to a European Union led policy.[26]

One thing Mihalka fails to address fully, which Cooley fleshes out in his 2012 look at Central Asia, is the importance of sovereignty to the Central Asian states, as well as to Russia and China. All of these states have a shared authoritarian style of government, and do not look kindly

---

[25]Michael D. Mihalka, "Not Much of a Game: Security Dynamics in Central Asia," *China and Eurasia Forum Quarterly* 5, no. 2 (May 2007), 1, http://www.silkroadstudies.org/new/docs/CEF/Quarterly/May_2007/Mihalka.pdf (accessed August 8, 2012), 21.

[26]Mihalka, 16.

on anything that threatens the stability of these regimes. This shared ideology precludes part of the realist use of balance of threat among these states, but does not prevent them from balancing against the "contagious ideology" of the United States.[27]

Alexander Cooley's 2012 *Great Games, Local Rules* completes the United States' shift toward truly looking at what drives the regimes of Central Asia, and how the United States can more successfully interact with them. He starts with the basis for the governmental model in Soviet history, describing the current model as "patrimonial," where leaders maintain position by distributing resources to a network of supportive political clients, something loosely shared with Russia and China.[28] This leads to Cooley's central thesis, that the United States must better understand how these "patrimonial" leaders work to maintain their power, and find ways to work within the "local rules" that they set rather than viewing the region top-down as the British and Russians did in Peter Hopkirk's *The Great Game*.[29]

Cooley argues that the United States' influence and interest in Central Asia are largely part of its larger interest in Afghanistan. Much of the security cooperation that the United States has done with Central Asia was to preclude radical Islamic uprisings in those states, with the added benefit to those regimes of helping to stamp out dissidents and human rights activists. This focus on security cooperation has come about largely because of the disproportionate application of military power in the region as part of the war in Afghanistan, as opposed to the more balanced national power strategies the United States might use during peacetime.

Cooley, even more so than Mihalka, uses the lens of realism to examine both the actions of the major powers with respect to each other and the Central Asian states, as well as the actions

---

[27]Walt, *America Unrivaled*, 137.

[28]Cooley, 17.

[29]Ibid., 5-6.

of the Central Asian states toward each other and the major powers. This look at both sides of the power equation in Central Asia is what the Chinese have been doing from the outset, seeking to understand how each side might mutually benefit, and how to avoid unproductive conflict. The United States has lagged behind in this approach, but as more authors recognize its importance, it should increasingly benefit the United States.

Common Themes in Central Asian International Relations

Throughout the writing of the major authors on international relations in Central Asia, one primary concept emerges. Except for some limited instances where liberal institutionalism is used, the predominant form of international relations thinking and action within Central Asia is realism. This lens holds true for interactions between the Central Asian states, the largely bilateral interactions between these states and the major powers, and in the direct interactions of the major powers themselves. None of the authors attempts to suggest that there is some collective ideal that can be acted upon through liberal institutionalism, because individual regime power and state sovereignty take precedence almost every time.

Once the major authors established that realism is the lens through which they view Central Asian international relations, as well as how the individual states generally view their actions and options, it becomes clear why the reoccurring themes spanning two decades of literature all seem decidedly self-serving. Security, economics, and energy are all common themes that at least seven of the nine major authors analyzed as part of the literature review. These themes play a pivotal role in how the major powers and Central Asian states interact, as each state has some interest in each of these.

However, not all of these are truly useful to study for the purpose of this monograph. The United States' economic interests in Central Asia are minimal at best, with little applicability to the current military power heavy form of United States' national power in Central Asia. For this reason, economics is not useful as a case study. While the same reasoning holds true for the use of energy, since none of the pipelines supply oil directly or indirectly to the United States, there is still competition by United States' companies to exploit Central Asian oil. Russia and China also still affect U.S. oil prices and energy security by competition for resources.

Finally, despite the fact that basing relates to security cooperation, it is given its own category because of its unique importance to United States' foreign policy in Central Asia. For the United States, basing is largely separate from traditional security cooperation, focused both on maintaining operational reach into Afghanistan and on maintaining an enduring presence in Central Asia. This minimal enduring presence, according to Mihalka and Cooley, is preferable to leaving the region altogether and then having to reestablish a presence if the security situation deteriorates. Conversely, they believe this minimal presence is all that the United States should maintain, both to avoid antagonizing Russia and China, and to avoid giving the individual Central Asian states impetus to balance against the United States.

Now that a review of a spectrum of Central Asian international relations literature has highlighted the various authors' views, the following table condenses this information into a clear picture of how the authors view the utility of realism and liberal institutionalism within Central Asia. The table places the authors' views against the three main categories for further study: security cooperation, energy, and basing. Where authors span multiple listings, the table lists them in all applicable areas.

Table 1: International relations theories and Central Asia major concerns, by author

	Realism	Liberal Institutionalism
	• Majority of actions will be bilateral (bandwagoning with major player to achieve goal) • States will balance threat from one major power by bandwagoning with another major power • Actions will be quid pro quo, benefitting both powers	• Majority of actions will be multilateral (common work toward common goal) • States will balance threat by forming a broad coalition against that threat • Actions benefit all partners, some more than others
Security Cooperation:	Brzezinski Naumkin Jonson Legvold Sultanov/Muzaparova Guangcheng Karrar Mihalka Cooley	Legvold Mihalka
Energy	Brzezinski Naumkin Sultanov/Muzaparova Guangcheng Karrar Mihalka Cooley	Mihalka
Basing	Naumkin Jonson Legvold Guangcheng Karrar Mihalka Cooley	Legvold Mihalka

CASE STUDIES

Methodology and Selection

The literature review identified a number of common subjects within Central Asia for exploration. This section must develop the content and scope of the case studies, which will more fully explore some selected areas of the common subjects. Two types of observational studies are possible: qualitative and quantitative.[30] Quantitative methods using a large number of similar

phenomena, with the same independent and dependent variables and not containing extraneous

variables, provide an excellent statistical analysis of the correlation between the variables.[31] If

certain variables are missing, or other extraneous variables are present, the researcher can conduct

other tests to consider this. The greatest problem with quantitative studies is that they require a

large amount of data, something not present for Central Asia due to its limited history on the

international stage and its generally understudied nature.

Qualitative methods using case studies require significantly less overall data to conduct.

They are both more decisive, because of their limited scope, and better explain how the variables

interact within the observation. This "process tracing" is important to identify and understand any

intervening variables, which allows a better understanding of overall causality.[32] It is for these

reasons that this monograph will use case studies to explore the relationships between the major

players, the Central Asian states, and the intervening variables seen in the various government

personalities of these states.

As the literature review has already highlighted, there are three common areas of concern

within Central Asia: security, economics, and energy. However, these broad categories cover too

much information for concise case studies. In order to make the case studies manageable within

the scope of this monograph, it is necessary to narrow their focus. To do this, it is easiest to focus

on only one of the Central Asian states. This focus permits a narrow enough amount of

---

[30]Stephen Van Evera, *Guide to Methods for Students of Political Science* (Ithaca: Cornell University Press, 1997), 3-4.

[31]Ibid., 51.

[32]Van Evera, 54.

observations to study effectively, while still allowing a wide enough view of the three major players interacting within that state.

Kazakhstan is the best state to use to develop case studies for a number of reasons. Its location, producing long borders with both Russia and China, forces it to interact with these two major players on a regular basis, for security, economic, and energy reasons. Likewise, its oil reserves are significantly higher than any other Central Asian state, giving more opportunities to explore how it uses energy as one way to balance against others' power.[33] These oil reserves and the major powers bordering it give Kazakhstan more bargaining ability than some of the other Central Asian states possess. Finally, Kazakhstan has had a stable government for its entire existence, with Nursultan Nazarbayev remaining as its president since independence in 1991. This long-term stability allows a better study of interactions between Kazakhstan and the major powers, as it does not introduce the variable of another government figure, not to mention the ensuing chaos of a government overthrow as happened in Kyrgyzstan in 2010.

Kazakhstan is not, however, the best fit to study everything suggested in the literature review. Economically, Kazakhstan's largest trading partner in 2011 was China, taking 21.7% of Kazakhstan's exports and providing 30.1% of its imports. In the same year, Russia provided a market for 5.3% of Kazakhstan's exports, while providing 20% of its imports.[34] Both Russia and China are in the top five trading partners for Kazakhstan, and together provide over half of Kazakhstan's imports. In contrast, Kazakhstan is the United States' 71st highest export partner,

---

[33]British Petroleum, *BP Statistical Review of World Energy: June 2012* (London: British Petroleum, 2012), 8, http://www.bp.com/liveassets/bp_internet/globalbp/globalbp_uk_english/reports_and_publications/statistical_energy_review_2011/STAGING/local_assets/pdf/statistical_review_of_world_energy_full_report_2012.pdf (accessed March 18, 2013).

[34]Central Intelligence Agency, "Central Asia: Kazakhstan," The World Factbook, https://www.cia.gov/library/publications/the-world-factbook/geos/kz.html (accessed March 18, 2013).

and 84th highest import partner. Because this monograph must have operational relevance to United States' planners, any case studies it contains must as well. As a result, because of its lack of proximity to the United States to conduct trade, and its low overall position in the United States' rank of trading partners, economics is not a good fit for a case study.

Likewise, nor are the major categories suggested by the literature review sufficient to help explain United States' influence in Central Asia, and Central Asia's reactions to that influence. While security cooperation between Kazakhstan and the major players provides a good fit, a subset provides a more in-depth analysis of United States' interaction within the region. That subset is basing. While basing as a general concept includes Russia, making the topic able to explore both Russian and United States' interaction with Central Asia, it is especially pertinent to United States Army planners, as it is one of the elements of operational art.[35] However, because of a lack of United States' basing in Kazakhstan, the basing case study must use Kyrgyzstan and Uzbekistan to explore the subject fully. While this introduces more than one Central Asian state into a case study, it effectively limits the major player variable to the United States, allowing a better study of how different states react to the United States.

All three of these case studies meet Van Evera's data-rich criteria.[36] Energy and security both have sufficient interactions between Kazakhstan as the focal point, the three major players, and the remainder of the Central Asian states to understand what international relations lens the government of Kazakhstan tends to use, and what approach has worked best in the past with it. Likewise, using the United States as the focal point for a basing study, along with the

---

[35]United States Army, *Army Doctrine Reference Publication ADRP 5-0: The Operations Process* (Washington: Department of the Army, 2012), 2-4.

[36]Van Evera, 78.

governments of Uzbekistan and Kyrgyzstan, provides the ability to compare and contrast United States' policies in these two countries and the effect they had on basing there.

In the table below are the predictors associated with the realist and liberal institutionalist lenses, which the energy, security cooperation, and basing case studies will examine in depth. An analysis of these case studies will help to explain how the relationships between the Central Asian states and the major powers work, and will lead to a prediction of effective future approaches in the conclusion.

Table 2: Predictors of international relations theories and Central Asia major concerns

	• Majority of actions will be bilateral (bandwagoning with major player to achieve goal) • States will balance threat from one major power by bandwagoning with another major power • Actions will be quid pro quo, benefitting both powers	• Majority of actions will be multilateral (common work toward common goal) • States will balance threat by forming a broad coalition against that threat • Actions benefit all partners, some more than others
	Realism	**Liberal Institutionalism**
Security Cooperation:		
Energy		
Basing		

Case Study 1: Kazakhstan's Military/Security Engagements

Since its independence, security has been a major concern for all of the Central Asian states, especially Kazakhstan. Externally, Kazakhstan borders both Russia and China, both extremely powerful neighbors with interests in Kazakhstan's internal workings, as Kazakhstan's stability affects the stability of their border regions. Likewise, internal security has been a strong interest for the Kazakh government under President Nursultan Nazarbayev, both in overall terms of the country's stability and more precisely because of regime preservation. Nazarbayev's rule has been termed "enlightened authoritarianism;" while he works to maintain his regime, he also introduces reforms that make Kazakhstan more like a democracy than it was under Soviet rule, and engenders increased trust in the local populace that the government is doing what is best for the nation as a whole.[37]

While Kazakhstan's enduring security concerns are primarily internal, they started out much more external. Upon its initial independence, Kazakhstan sought to maintain the nuclear weapons, including intercontinental ballistic missiles, remaining on its territory from the Soviet Union. However, Kazakhstan soon discovered that security and upkeep of these weapons and facilities was beyond their capability, and that the weapons did not truly give them the deterrent capability they desired. As a result, they repatriated all of the nuclear warheads to Russia by 1995, and dismantled the testing facility at Semipalatinsk by 2000.

Likewise, they participated with the United States in PROJECT SAPPHIRE, which transferred over 600 kilograms of highly enriched uranium to the United States.[38] This supported the United States' non-proliferation policy, and gained the Kazakh government $27,000,000 at a time when its economy was rapidly deteriorating.[39] On both non-proliferation accounts, getting rid of nuclear material to a state better able to safeguard it removed a security headache for Kazakhstan and allowed it to focus its efforts elsewhere. The bilateral nature of both transfers of nuclear material indicates the beginning of strong realist trend in security cooperation.

Beyond PROJECT SAPPHIRE, the United States' initial interest in security cooperation with Kazakhstan was minimal. However, the Russians maintained an interest in security

---

[37]Pavel K. Baev, "Turning Counter-Terrorism Into Counter-Revolution: Russia Focuses On Kazakhstan and Engages Turkmenistan," *European Security* 15, no. 1 (March 2006), 13.

[38]John A. Tirpak, "Project Sapphire," airforce-magazine.com, http://www.airforce-magazine.com/MagazineArchive/Pages/1995/August%201995/0895sapphire.aspx (accessed March 19, 2013).

[39]David E. Hoffmann, "Half a Ton of Uranium -- and a Long Flight," *Washington Post*, September 21, 2009. http://articles.washingtonpost.com/2009-09-21/world/36894943_1_enrichment-level-uranium-nuclear-materials (accessed March 19, 2013).

cooperation with their former republics in Central Asia, especially with Kazakhstan, as it is the only Central Asian State directly bordering Russia.[40] One of the Russians' major concerns was that, if radical Islam gained a foothold in Central Asia, it might destabilize Islamic minority groups living within Russia's borders.[41] Other factors driving Russia's attempts to maintain stability amongst the former republics included maintaining prestige amongst the former Soviet states, the inherently interconnected economic systems of Russia and the former republics, and concern for the border region buffer beyond the spread of radical Islam.[42]

All of these concerns prompted the Russians to establish the Commonwealth of Independent States (CIS) on December 8, 1991.[43] However, the CIS focuses primarily on economic and trade issues among the former Russian republics. While improved economic collaboration fosters better security throughout the region due to increased satisfaction of the populations with their respective governments, the CIS does not focus directly on security issues, thus prompting the next logical step in Russia's involvement with its former republics, the formation of the Collective Security Treaty Organization (CSTO).[44] A military alliance between Armenia, Belarus, Kazakhstan, Kyrgyzstan, Russia, and Tajikistan created the CSTO on May 15, 1992.

At the beginning, the CSTO was primarily a Russian construct. However, Russian involvement has varied since 1992, and the CSTO has become much more than just an

---

[40]Brzezinski, chap. 4, under "Russia's new Geopolitical Setting."

[41]Cooley, 24.

[42]Ibid., 58.

[43]Brzezinski, chap. 4, under "Russia's New Geopolitical Setting."

[44]Collective Security Treaty Organization, "Organization of the Collective Security Treaty," The Collective Security Treaty Organization, http://www.odkb.gov.ru/start/index_aengl.htm (accessed March 20, 2013).

epiphenomenal institutional shell. This change is apparent in the rotating nature of the CSTO

chairmanship, which provides all of the member states a turn at guiding the CSTO for the period

of one year.[45] While Russia is undeniably the most powerful among the member states, the

rotating chairmanship gives member states increased stake in problem solving and making the

organization truly multilateral, rather than each state simply working bilaterally with only

Russia.[46]

Increased multilateralism is also visible with the creation of the Collective Rapid

Reaction Forces (KSOR) in 2009.[47] The CSTO council controls this multilateral peacekeeping

unit, designed for operations within the CSTO member nations. Its employment was originally

dependent on consensus among the CSTO council members, but this changed in 2010 to allow a

majority ballot to authorize its use.[48] While this detracts somewhat from the breadth of

multilateralism in this organization, it does not undermine the multilateral nature of the KSOR

itself. This change actually increases the likelihood that the KSOR can and will be used in the

future for the good of the majority of the CSTO.

While security engagement centered on Russia and the CSTO has become increasingly

multilateral, military engagement under the auspices of the SCO remains largely bilateral,

although recent exercises indicate minimally increased multilateralism. The SCO, originally

---

[45]Roger N. McDermott, *The Kazakhstan-Russia Axis: Shaping CSTO Transformation* (Fort Leavenworth: Foreign Military Studies Office, 2011), 5-6, http://fmso.leavenworth.army.mil/Collaboration/international/McDermott/CSTO_Transformation -final.pdf (accessed March 20, 2013).

[46]Jason P. Davis and Kathleen M. Eisenhardt, "Rotating Leadership and Collaborative Innovation: Recombination Processes in Symbiotic Relationships," *Administrative Science Quarterly* 56, no. 2 (June 2011), 3.

[47]McDermott, 3. KSOR comes from the Russian *Kollektivnyye Sily Operativnogo Reagirovaniya*, not the English title.

[48]McDermott, 4.

formed informally as the "Shanghai 5" in 1996, is a loose cooperative grouping of China, Russia, Kazakhstan, Kyrgyzstan, and Tajikistan.[49] Uzbekistan joined the group in 2001. The SCO was formalized with a charter in 2002, settling on a liberal institutionalist structure, if perhaps not its content.

As an essayist at Sweden's Linköping University adroitly states, the SCO is fixated on "safeguarding sovereignty, instead of sovereignty-pooling."[50] This lack of multilateralism is largely due to the requirement of authoritarian Central Asian governments for regime preservation. This requirement plays out in evolving military cooperation among members of the SCO. Originally, the SCO was nothing more than a forum for discussion of common issues, with any agreements made either outside of the SCO, or as bilateral agreements between China and one of the Central Asian nations. One such example of this is the border dispute between China and Kazakhstan, a holdover from the disputed border of the USSR. While the SCO served as a vehicle for discussion of border militarization in general among its members, the actual treaty was bilaterally resolved outside of the organization itself.

Today, while the SCO still serves primarily as a meeting ground for its members to discuss common security issues, it has begun to take on limited multilateralism. Beginning in 2003, the SCO has held multilateral exercises every few years, three of which have involved Kazakhstan.[51] These three exercises focused exclusively on anti-terrorism, a catchall term in Central Asia that includes traditional terrorism, separatism, and dissent activities. Because of the

---

[49]Andrew Scheineson, "The Shanghai Cooperation Organization," Council on Foreign Relations, http://www.cfr.org/international-peace-and-security/shanghai-cooperation-organization/p10883 (accessed March 20, 2013).

[50]Hossein Aghaie Joobani, "The Shanghai Cooperation Organization in Light of Organization Theory," e-International Relations, http://www.e-ir.info/2013/02/22/the-shanghai-cooperation-organization-in-light-of-organization-theory/ (accessed March 20, 2013).

[51]PLA Daily.

regimes' emphasis on self-preservation, these exercises significantly increase their self-preservation capabilities. However, despite the fact that the training is multilateral, it still falls back on Joobani's concept of safeguarding, rather than pooling, sovereignty.[52] The application of new skills obtained during training is solely the purview of the individual states, not the SCO as a whole.

While the CSTO has moved well along the path to multilateralism, and the SCO has begun to make modest inroads in multilateral military cooperation, the United Nations and NATO focused multilateral attempts have taken a step backward. The Central Asia Battalion (CENTRAZBAT), developed in 1995, was nominally a multinational peacekeeping battalion, with companies from Kazakhstan, Kyrgyzstan, and Uzbekistan.[53] It conducted its first military exercises in 1997, and included forces from five other countries, including the United States and Russia. In 2000, CENTRAZBAT expanded to include full battalions from its member nations, a move aimed at increasing capability. The Kazakh contribution to this effort was KAZBAT, a motorized battalion designed for peacekeeping operations.[54] Internal differences between the three CENTRAZBAT members caused the organization to dissolve in 2002.

However, KAZBAT continued as a Kazakh peacekeeping formation, and began to conduct exercises both as part of CSTO with Russia starting in 2002 with COMMONWEALTH SOUTHERN SHIELD, and with the United States and the United Kingdom starting in 2003 with

---

[52]Joobani.

[53]Kenley Butler, "U.S. Military Cooperation with the Central Asian States," James Martin Center for Nonproliferation Studies, http://cns.miis.edu/archive/wtc01/uscamil.htm (accessed April 3, 2013).

[54]Matthew Stein, *Compendium of Central Asian Military and Security Activity* (Fort Leavenworth: Foreign Military Studies Office, 2012), 13, http://fmso.leavenworth.army.mil/documents/Central-Asian-Military-Events.pdf (accessed March 20, 2013).

Steppe Eagle.[55] Steppe Eagle occurred annually since then, generally in September. However, the Kazakh government pushed it one month earlier in 2010 to avoid conflict with a Chinese exercise.[56] For most of the Steppe Eagle exercises, there was no attempt to involve other Central Asian states in cooperation or partnership. There was also continual delay in developing both a full brigade of peacekeepers (KAZBRIG), as well as inter-operational capability with NATO. Both of these were due either to use of resources elsewhere or because of desire to gain training value without having to contribute as part of a liberal democratic institution.

However, as of Steppe Eagle 2011, there has been some added emphasis on multilateralism, adding soldiers from Lithuania and Kyrgyzstan to the exercise. Although these countries participated, the exercise lacked the true multinational effort afforded to the CSTO's KSOR efforts. Instead, it is more on par with the SCO's military cooperation efforts, which gain each individual participant skills at a collective training event that they then apply at home.

Throughout this case study, Kazakhstan's military engagements have split between realist and liberal institutionalist tendencies. Its interactions with China and the United States have been primarily bilateral, with early United States led multilateral efforts with CENTRAZBAT having failed by the early 2000s. The few remaining multilateral exercises exhibit no true cooperation beyond collective training opportunities. These training opportunities do not promote the multilateral forces interoperable as part of a liberal institution, but merely provide an

---

[55]Stein, 12-20.

[56]Author's personal observations as part of the ARCENT exercise staff for Operation Steppe Eagle 2009 and 2010; PLA Daily. One of the ARCENT G-7 (Training and Exercise) personnel indicated to the author that Steppe Eagle had been moved up a month to avoid conflict with a Chinese exercise. The PLA Daily site indicates a SCO exercise in September, which is the month in which Kazakhstan hosted Steppe Eagle 2009. As a result, NATO's Steppe Eagle 2010 was moved a month earlier to August, at the request of the Kazakh government.

epiphenomenal vehicle to share knowledge that the participants then use solely for individual sovereignty protection.

This is not true for Kazakh interactions conducted through the Russian-dominated CSTO, which more closely aligns with liberal institutionalism. In this organization, all parties have worked to improve KSOR's collective forces, which help to ensure collective security, or at least collective regime preservation. While each state still focuses on its own sovereignty, there is still much more cooperation than is evident with either Chinese or United States led organizations.

Case Study 2: Kazakhstan as an Energy Provider

With proven oil reserves of at least 30 billion barrels, the largest reserve in Central Asia by a wide margin, Kazakhstan holds 1.8% of the earth's oil reserves.[57] Foreign and domestic oil companies discovered 82% of these reserves since 2001. The recentness of these discoveries accounts for Kazakhstan's high reserves to production ratio, a measure of how long current reserves will last at current production, as infrastructure to extract and transport oil takes a significant amount of time to construct. As of 2011, Kazakhstan produced 2.1% of the world's oil, with the ability to sustain production at this rate for at least the next 44 years.[58] This long-term viability of Kazakhstan's oil production makes large, long lead-time pipeline projects feasible, as production will continue long enough and at a high enough rate to recoup the pipeline costs.

Kazakhstan's oil infrastructure build-up since independence accounts for much of the production capacity it has today.[59] Foreign investment, primarily from the United States, Russia,

---

[57]British Petroleum, 6.

[58]British Petroleum, 8.

[59]U.S. Energy Information Administration, *Kazakhstan* (Washington: U.S. Energy Information Administration, 2012),

33

and China, built most of this production infrastructure. However, since 2002, Kazakhstan's national oil and gas company, KazMunaiGaz (KMG) has competed with foreign investors for contracts, serving to keep profits from exploration and extraction of oil and natural gas within the borders of Kazakhstan itself. As of 2012, the Kazakh government reserves a majority portion of any new project for KMG, keeping economic development within the country and decreasing reliance on foreign expertise. This realist approach shows that Kazakhstan's government is sensitive to increasing its own economic capacity, and in doing so by mitigating potentially disruptive foreign influence.

Kazakhstan did not start its independent existence with much in the way of oil export infrastructure. Initially, the only pipeline leaving this landlocked nation went northwest into Russia from Atyrau, Kazakhstan to Samara, Russia.[60] This kept Kazakhstan tied to Russia for all of its energy export capability for the first fifteen years of its independence, until KMG and the China National Petroleum Corporation (CNPC) completed the oil pipeline to China on December 21, 2005.[61] This pipeline finally gave Kazakhstan options with its energy sales, allowing it to better balance against demands from either Russia or China, as well as allowing it to prevent an embargo by either from completely shutting down a major source of national income. Both of these outcomes support Kazakhstan's realist tendencies, as they look after their own self-interests.

---

http://www.eia.gov/countries/analysisbriefs/Kazakhstan/kazakhstan.pdf (accessed March 18, 2013).

[60]Ariel K. Cohen, *U.S. Interests and Central Asia Energy Security* (Washington: The Heritage Foundation, 2006), 3, http://www.policyarchive.org/handle/10207/bitstreams/11895.pdf (accessed March 18, 2013).

[61]China National Petroleum Company, "Major Events 2006," China National Petroleum Company, http://www.cnpc.com.cn/eng/company/presentation/history/MajorEvents/2006.htm (accessed January 25, 2013).

Kazakhstan's oil export routes are of little direct concern to the United States. However, Kazakhstan's stature as a major oil producer is. Kazakhstan is a not a member of the twelve-state Organization of the Petroleum Exporting Countries (OPEC).[62] This by itself is not significant, but coupled with the fact that Kazakhstan is the world's 18th largest oil producer and 14th largest oil exporter, Kazakhstan's lack of OPEC membership gives it and any energy consumers closely allied with it leverage against price and production controls that OPEC might levy against its member nations.[63] This further highlights Kazakhstan's realist nature, as it has not joined any liberal institutions such as OPEC, which would constrain its energy actions. While this may have hurt Kazakhstan's ability to move its oil to market, it also protects Kazakhstan's sovereignty and gives it the ability to bandwagon with one or more of the major powers against OPEC in times of crisis.

This ability to act as a counterweight to OPEC is one of the United States' primary interests in Kazakhstan's energy arena, beyond competition by United States' companies to explore and extract Kazakh oil.[64] Unlike Russia and China, there is no direct pipeline from Kazakhstan to the United States, necessarily making any United States' energy interest of an indirect nature. Kazakhstan's influence on the overall world price of oil, especially its ability to influence non-OPEC prices, makes it important for price stability of oil for the United States and its allies. Because the United States has no direct energy tie to Kazakhstan, however, any positive

---

[62]Organization of the Petroleum Exporting Countries, "Member Countries," Organization of the Petroleum Exporting Countries, http://www.opec.org/opec_web/en/about_us/25.htm (accessed March 18, 2013).

[63]Kimberly Martin, *Disrupting the Balance: Russian Efforts to Control Kazakhstan's Oil* (New York: Columbia University - Barnard College, 2006), 2, http://csis.org/files/media/csis/pubs/pm_0428.pdf (accessed March 18, 2013).

[64]Philip K. Verleger, *Adjusting to Volatile Energy Prices* (Washington: Peterson Institute, 1994), 184.

influence must come from other portions of national power, as is apparent with the two nations' military and security cooperation ties. These help stabilize Kazakhstan, thus keeping prices lower for everyone, which is in the United States' best interest.

Throughout this case study, Kazakhstan's energy policies have been strictly realist. All of Kazakhstan's current pipelines are bilateral agreements with either Russia or China, with quid pro quo being oil for money to fuel Kazakhstan's economy. Much of this is because of the proximity of Russia and China, both of which border Kazakhstan, as well as Kazakhstan's landlocked nature. However, there are other outlets for pipelines, but each of these outlets requires going through multiple countries to reach a terminal to export the oil. While these are still being considered and actively planned for, liberal institutionalist cooperation and partnerships to export oil are taking a significant amount of time for Kazakhstan to develop.

Case Study 3: United States' Basing in Central Asia—Uzbekistan vs. Kyrgyzstan

While the United States has true strategic reach, and is able to support operations throughout the world, it does require partnerships with other nations to achieve this reach. Basing, a key component of operational art, is necessary to allow strategic and operational reach.[65] These bases allow United States Transportation Command (TRANSCOM) to move personnel, equipment, and other supplies effectively. Within a landlocked area such as Central Asia, air bases are the primary means to facilitate this flow.[66] Thus, when the United States found itself faced with the prospect of conducting operations in Afghanistan, itself a landlocked nation just south of Central Asia, it turned to the Central Asian states for help.

---

[65]United States Army, *ADRP 5-0*, 2-4.

[66]The United States refers to Manas as a "transit center" in an attempt to remove a military connotation from their operations there.

The United States signed the first such agreement with Uzbekistan on October 7, 2001, which allowed United States' troops to use Karshi-Khanabad (K2) for operations in Afghanistan.[67] In return, Uzbekistan received security guarantees from the United States to target Islamic Movement of Uzbekistan (IMU) terrorist forces, as well as a tacit agreement to overlook human rights violations.[68] Uzbekistan allowed the United States to put up to 1500 troops at the base, with the inner security cordon composed of United States' forces, and use the base to stage fixed and rotary-wing assets. During initial operations, the base served a primarily operational role, staging assets employed directly against the Taliban and Al Qaida. However, over the next few years, it focused more strategically, allowing TRANSCOM C-17 cargo traffic to transit onward into Afghanistan.

The United States – Uzbekistan partnership at K2 ended not long after the Andijan protests of May 12-13, 2005. Uzbek security forces met these protests by Uzbek citizens against the repressions and corruption of the Uzbek government with violent reprisals, resulting in hundreds of protestors dead. Despite the 2001 tacit agreement to the contrary, the United States' government voiced strong criticisms of the Uzbek government.[69] As a result, Uzbekistan initially curtailed United States' operations at K2, limiting overflight permissions and the types of supplies that the United States could move through K2. This curtailment forced the United States to move much of its operational assets to Kandahar, and further pushed strategic lift assets to

---

[67]Jim Nichol, *Uzbekistan's Closure of the Airbase at Karshi-Khanabad: Context and Implications* (Washington: Congressional Research Service, 2005), 1, http://digital.library.unt.edu/ark:/67531/metacrs7519/m1/1/high_res_d/RS22295_2005Oct07.pdf (accessed March 20, 2013).

[68]Ibid., 1-2.

[69]Walt, *America Unrivaled*, 137.

Manas in Kyrgyzstan. Uzbekistan chose to terminate the United States' lease soon after curtailment, with United States' forces having 180 days to clear out of K2.

It is no surprise that the following year Uzbekistan joined the CSTO, putting it squarely in a multilateral agreement with Russia and the other CSTO members.[70] This move is a significant balance of threat policy shift against the "contagious ideology" of the United States, whose liberal democracy and human rights agenda works directly against the authoritarian regime in Uzbekistan. Uzbekistan rightfully feels that bandwagoning with Russia and other like autocratic regimes, for the purpose of regime preservation, is in the best interest of its government.[71]

The United States began operations at Manas in December 2001, with much the same initial agreement as it had developed months earlier with Uzbekistan.[72] Because of its distance from Afghanistan, compared to K2 and airfields within Afghanistan itself, Manas has always remained more important for strategic rather than operational reach. Manas' importance increased significantly when Uzbekistan evicted the United States from K2 in 2005, becoming the United States' sole air hub in Central Asia.

By 2009, the Kyrgyz government had begun to receive a large amount of pressure from Russia to remove the United States from Manas. In February 2009, the Kyrgyz government asked the United States to leave, an act that garnered them approximately $2 billion in Russian aid.[73]

---

[70]Rustam Burnashev and Irina Chernykh, "Changes in Uzbekistan's Military Policy After the Andijan Events," *China and Eurasia Forum Quarterly* (February 2007), 72.

[71]Walt, *America Unrivaled*, 137.

[72]United States Air Force, "Fact Sheets," Transit Center at Manas, http://www.manas.afcent.af.mil/library/factsheets/index.asp (accessed March 22, 2013).

[73]Sabah Aslam, "Kyrgyzstan: Internal Instability and Revolt in 2010," *Strategic Studies* (Spring 2011), 253.

However, instead of following through on their threat, they merely renegotiated the United States' contract from $17.4 million to $60 million, plus significant upgrades to Manas Airport.[74]

On April 6-7, 2010, the people of Kyrgyzstan conducted a popular uprising against President Bakiyev's government, which had ruled since an earlier uprising in 2005.[75] Although some in the media felt that this was the result of Russian interference following Kyrgyzstan's 2009 actions, this social unrest was primarily the Kyrgyz public's reaction to President Bakiyev's poor governance and corruption. This unrest temporarily interrupted fuel shipments to Manas, forcing the United States to use other facilities temporarily throughout United States Central Command (CENTCOM) area of responsibility. Within a week, however, flights through the Manas Transit Center were back to normal.

How did the United States avoid eviction from Kyrgyzstan when it could not in Uzbekistan five years earlier? Multiple realist reasons lend themselves to the United States' staying power in Kyrgyzstan. First, despite the large influx of Russian aid, Kyrgyzstan's government was quite happy to have a second source of income, a quid pro quo for our use of Manas. The threat of closure of this important base merely increased the amount the United States was willing to pay to maintain it. Another reason was a lack of credible United States' threat to the Kyrgyz regime, both before and after the unrest. The United States voiced minimal concern over Kyrgyzstan's human rights, democracy, or free market economy issues. This muted opposition was due to the United States having learned that the autocratic regimes that govern Central Asia perceive such comments as promoting a contagious ideology, which then caused

---

[74]Aslam, 255.

[75]Jim Nichol, *The April 2010 Coup in Kyrgyzstan and Its Aftermath* (Washington: Congressional Research Service, 2010), under "Summary," http://www.dtic.mil/cgi-bin/GetTRDoc?Location=U2&doc=GetTRDoc.pdf&AD=ADA523588 (accessed March 20, 2013).

these regimes to balance against this threat.[76] In the case of the 2010 regime change, the new government also had nothing to hold against the United States even if there had been commentary, as the unrest had removed the old regime. Ultimately, because the unrest and subsequent regime change did not stem directly from United States' involvement, but instead Bakiyev's lack of enlightenment and Kyrgyzstan's governmental corruption, the United States retained its lease at Manas.

CASE STUDY ANALYSIS

The previous case studies examined three of the most important international relations issues in Central Asia. While these do not match exactly with the major topics derived from a review of Central Asian international relations literature, they do follow these topics closely, and provide for an examination of issues more pertinent to United States' operational planners than the originally suggested topics.

Throughout the military engagement case study, Kazakhstan's military engagements split between realist and liberal institutionalist tendencies. Its interactions with China and the United States have been primarily bilateral. Early United States led multilateral efforts with CENTRAZBAT failed by the early 2000s, and the few remaining multilateral exercises as part of the SCO exhibit no true cooperation beyond collective training opportunities. The same is not true for interactions conducted through the Russian-led CSTO, which align much more closely with liberal institutionalism. In this organization, all parties have worked to improve KSOR's collective forces to help to ensure collective security, or at least collective regime preservation. While each state still focuses on its own sovereignty, there is still much more cooperation than is evident with either Chinese or United States led organizations.

---

[76]Walt, *America Unrivaled*, 137.

40

Within the energy case study, Kazakhstan's policies to date have been realist. All of Kazakhstan's current pipelines flow to either Russia or China, exchanging oil for cash, which fuels Kazakhstan's economy. The bilateral nature of this exchange is due to the geographic proximity of Russia and China, as well as Kazakhstan's landlocked nature. While there are other outlets for pipelines, these outlets require going through multiple countries to reach a terminal to export the oil. Kazakhstan and its neighbors are still exploring these options; however, liberal institutionalist cooperation and partnerships to export oil are taking a long time to develop.[77]

Finally, the basing case study highlights another aspect of realism that has implications for any United States' interactions in Central Asia. In Uzbekistan, the United States' commentary on human rights abuses was diametrically opposed to the authoritarian regime in power. This regime, in an effort to protect itself against this contagious ideology, chose to balance against this threat by limiting United States' access, terminating the Karshi-Khanabad Airbase lease.[78] This contrasts with the United States' experience in Kyrgyzstan where, despite significant attempts by the Russians to entice the Kyrgyz government to sever the Manas Transit Center contract, the United States prevailed in keeping a base. In this instance, the United States muted its criticisms, thereby avoiding Kyrgyzstan seeing it as an ideological threat. The United States also significantly increased its rent payment, another realist move through quid pro quo.

All three case studies highlight a primarily realist tendency for the current regimes in Central Asia. Realism is visible first through the primarily bilateral security cooperation agreements that they conduct with China and the United States. Although both of these programs contain some form of multilateralism, it is at best an epiphenomenon, as the substance of the cooperation lasts only as long as the training exercises. This bilateralism is also visible in the

---

[77]Verleger, 184.

[78]Walt, *America Unrivaled*, 137.

pipeline politics of Kazakhstan, where pipelines, and therefore oil agreements, exist only with Russia and China. The fact that Kazakhstan has oil pipelines to two major countries allows it to bandwagon with either in time of crisis without cutting all oil revenue, reinforcing its realist tendencies. Finally, basing shows both the power of money in quid pro quo efforts to buy influence in the region, and its limitations when it is unable to overcome a Central Asian State balancing against the threat of the United States' "contagious ideology."[79]

However, there are some surprising areas of liberal institutionalism. This tendency manifests itself most strongly in Central Asia's dealings with Russia through the CSTO, as well as with limited instances in its actions with China through the SCO and the actions of the former CENTRAZBAT nations with the United States. The CSTO phenomenon shows that the Central Asian states are willing to work closely, even cede some limited sovereignty, in a group with like government regimes. In this case, they are most comfortable, and ideologically aligned, with Russia. This comfort level does not hold true with the United States, thus one of the reasons for the dissolution of CENTRAZBAT, and the primarily bilateral agreements seen since with the United States.

The following table highlights the various realist and liberal institutionalist tendencies seen in the case studies. The security cooperation and energy case studies focus on Kazakhstan, but the answers extend to the other Central Asian states. The basing case study applies even more broadly across Central Asia, and highlights how differing ideologies can cause Central Asian states to balance against others.

---

[79]Walt, *America Unrivaled*, 137.

	Majority of actions will be bilateral (bandwagoning with major player to achieve goal) • States will balance threat from one major power by bandwagoning with another major power • Actions will be quid pro quo, benefitting both powers	• Majority of actions will be multilateral (common work toward common goal) • States will balance threat by forming a broad coalition against that threat • Actions benefit all partners, some more than others
	Realism	**Liberal Institutionalism**
Security Cooperation:	+ failure of CENTRAZBAT (failure of multinationalism) + creation of KAZBAT (bilateral work with major powers, but neither a coalition of major powers nor coalition of Central Asian states) + common security, but enacted only bilaterally, not multilaterally	+ CSTO, through KSOR, does enable multilateral common and collective security - SCO has the form of a liberal institution, provides forum for discussion of interests, but does not enable multilateral cooperation among major players and/or Central Asian states
Energy	+ Pipelines to Russia and China benefit only Kazakhstan (bilateral, quid pro quo) + China pipeline balance of threat against possible blockade by Russia + multiple pipelines provide options in the future to balance threat by either Russia or China	- pipelines outside of Russia and China are only proposals at this point
Basing	+ Quid pro quo (monetary payment by US for access) + denial of basing despite monetary compensation based on balance of threat (US liberal democratic ideology vs. authoritarian Central Asian regimes)	- Central Asian states vie amongst themselves for money by selling access; no common interest

CONCLUSIONS

Now that the case study analysis has highlighted the differences in how Central Asia

deals with each of the three major powers, as well as their primarily realist outlook on

international relations in general, what does this mean for the future of United States' interactions

with Central Asia? Specifically, what implications does this knowledge of Central Asia's realist

tendencies have for operational planners at CENTCOM and ARCENT, who must work to

develop and implement the military portion of United States' national power within the region?

Primarily, operational planners must realize that, although in overall international relations the United States is the largest player, for Central Asia the United States is a distant third due to proximity and habitual influence. Russia maintains primacy for Central Asia among the three major powers, both because of its proximity and because of the habitual relationship with the Central Asian states begun when they were part of the USSR. China also maintains influence far above that of the United States, because of its proximity and thus its attendant economic, energy, and military cooperation with Central Asia.

Based on Mihalka and Cooley's arguments, the United States should conform to a minimalist strategy for interactions with Central Asia, but not a strategy of complete disengagement.[80] The Central Asian states are dealing effectively with most of the major threats that earlier authors identified at the turn of this century. Thus, while the United States does not stand to gain much by attempting to increase presence, due to the already high level of interaction between Central Asia, Russia, and China, it stands to lose whatever minimal influence it currently has to the other major powers through any further disengagement. This potential loss is particularly true of basing, which is relatively easy to keep once obtained, but much more difficult to regain once lost or given up.

However, in the absence of clear strategic guidance, operational planners must default to their own understanding of the strategic context in which they operate. In Central Asia, this means understanding the strategic context that the first four chapters of this monograph have laid out. As part of this context, operational planners must always remember that regime preservation is first among the many competing demands for the governments of Central Asia. Based on Balance of Threat theory, these governments are willing to work most closely with ideologically similar governments, while viewing those governments with differing views more suspiciously.

---

[80]Cooley, 163-177; Mihalka, 38-39.

This suspicion results in limited opportunities for the United States' partnership with the Central Asian states, and ensures that any cooperation will likely be limited in scope and bilateral in nature. In short, the status quo of exercises and information exchanges will continue largely unchanged in content, scope, and bilateral nature, as this presents a low threat to the Central Asian states and mutual benefit to both partners.

Army operational planners must ensure that any exercises and information exchanges they allocate resources to as part of CENTCOM's theater security cooperation program are of mutual benefit to both the United States and Kazakhstan.[81] Because of the Central Asian states' overt regard for regime preservation and stability, antiterrorism exercises have been and continue to be the most beneficial to them. While they may not benefit the United States in terms of knowledge gained, these exercises and information exchanges do benefit by maintaining contact between the two militaries, and by exposing other militaries to the United States in a less threatening way. Ultimately, this gives the United States' ties to the region if it needs to stabilize a deteriorating situation in the future.

Despite the United States' best efforts, Central Asia will not meet all of its proposed activities favorably. The Central Asian states will deny some efforts outright. Other efforts, like Steppe Eagle 2010, will move dates to accommodate activities with higher priority partners. United States' operational planners should actively take into account the activities of the other major players within Central Asia, and should deconflict competing interests. This deconfliction maximizes the United States' use of resources, and avoids needlessly irritating Russia and China, both of which carry more influence within Central Asia. Avoiding unnecessary problems with the

---

[81]United States Army, *Field Manual FM 3-22: Army Support to Security Cooperation* (Washington: Department of the Army, 2013), 1-6.

other major powers helps to ensure that they do not actively attempt to balance against the United States within Central Asia, which would further limit United States' power in the region.

During the research for this monograph, a number of other areas of study not directly part of the subject presented themselves for further study by other international relations and Central Asia scholars. The most closely linked to this monograph is a case study of problems associated with the Aral Sea diversion and desertification, a problem which plagues Kazakhstan and Uzbekistan, highlighting how the Central Asian states conduct relations amongst themselves without major power interference. Also closely linked to the region is a possible study on how the authoritarian Central Asian regimes will transfer power as their current generation of leaders reach retirement age. Finally, in a broader international relations focus, is a theme that reoccurred numerous times during research, with the relation of business and management models to liberal institutionalism. Research on any of these topics will further expand knowledge of the relatively understudied region of Central Asia.

Throughout this monograph, the reader has gained an understanding of why Kazakhstan is important within Central Asia, the issues important within the region, how the major powers interact in the region within these issues, and what all of this means for current and future operational planners. The strategic context underlying United States' actions in Central Asia is complex, and deserves further study by any operational planner assigned to the region.

BIBLIOGRAPHY

Aslam, Sabah. "Kyrgyzstan: Internal Instability and Revolt in 2010." *Strategic Studies* (Spring 2011): 241-261.

Baev, Pavel K. "Turning Counter-Terrorism Into Counter-Revolution: Russia Focuses On Kazakhstan and Engages Turkmenistan." *European Security* 15, no. 1 (March 2006): 3-22.

Bailes, Alyson J.K., Pal Dunay, Pan Guang, and Mikhail Troitskiy. *The Shanghai Cooperation Organization: SIPRI Policy Paper No. 17*. Stockholm: Stockholm International Peace Research Institute, 2007. http://www.voltairenet.org/IMG/pdf/SIPRI-Shangai_Coop_Org.pdf (accessed September 28, 2012).

Bartles, Charles K. *Challenges in Building Partner Capacities: Evaluating the Effectiveness of Security Assistance Programs in Kazakhstan*. Fort Leavenworth: Foreign Military Studies Office, 2012. http://fmso.leavenworth.army.mil/documents/challenges-building-partner-capacities.pdf (accessed August 8, 2012).

British Petroleum. *BP Statistical Review of World Energy: June 2012*. London: British Petroleum, 2012. http://www.bp.com/liveassets/bp_internet/globalbp/globalbp_uk_english/reports_and_pu blications/statistical_energy_review_2011/STAGING/local_assets/pdf/statistical_review_ of_world_energy_full_report_2012.pdf (accessed March 18, 2013).

Brzezinski, Zbigniew. *The Grand Chessboard: American Primacy and Its Geostrategic Imperatives*. New York: Basic Books, 1997. Kindle e-book.

Burnashev, Rustam, and Irina Chernykh. "Changes in Uzbekistan's Military Policy After the Andijan Events." *China and Eurasia Forum Quarterly* (February 2007): 67-73.

Butler, Kenley. "U.S. Military Cooperation with the Central Asian States." James Martin Center for Nonproliferation Studies. http://cns.miis.edu/archive/wtc01/uscamil.htm (accessed April 3, 2013).

Central Intelligence Agency. "Central Asia: Kazakhstan." The World Factbook. https://www.cia.gov/library/publications/the-world-factbook/geos/kz.html (accessed March 18, 2013).

China National Petroleum Company. "Major Events 2006." China National Petroleum Company. http://www.cnpc.com.cn/eng/company/presentation/history/MajorEvents/2006.htm (accessed January 25, 2013).

Cohen, Ariel K. *U.S. Interests and Central Asia Energy Security*. Washington: The Heritage Foundation, 2006. http://www.policyarchive.org/handle/10207/bitstreams/11895.pdf (accessed March 18, 2013).

Collective Security Treaty Organization. "Organization of the Collective Security Treaty." The Collective Security Treaty Organization. http://www.odkb.gov.ru/start/index_aengl.htm (accessed March 20, 2013).

Cooley, Alexander. *Great Games, Local Rules: The New Great Power Contest in Central Asia.* New York: Oxford University Press, 2012. Kindle e-book.

Davis, Jason P., and Kathleen M. Eisenhardt. "Rotating Leadership and Collaborative Innovation: Recombination Processes in Symbiotic Relationships." *Administrative Science Quarterly* 56, no. 2 (June 2011): 159-201.

Du, Ruoxi. *Kazakhstan: A Weakening Fiscal Regime under the New Ownership Structure?* Fort Leavenworth: Foreign Military Studies Office, 2012. http://fmso.leavenworth.army.mil/Collaboration/universities/Kazakhstan_DU_final.pdf (accessed August 8, 2012).

Garnett, Sherman W. "The Strategic Challenge of Kazakhstan and Inner Asia." In *Thinking Strategically: The Major Powers, Kazakhstan, and the Central Asian Nexus*, edited by Robert Legvold, 217-234. Cambridge: MIT Press, 2003.

George, Alexander L., and Andrew Bennett. *Case Studies and Theory Development in the Social Sciences.* Cambridge: MIT Press, 2005.

Grau, Lester W. *The Bear Went Over the Mountain: Soviet Combat Tactics in Afghanistan.* Washington: National Defense University Press, 1995.

Guangcheng, Xing "China's Foreign Policy Toward Kazakhstan." In *Thinking Strategically: The Major Powers, Kazakhstan, and the Central Asian Nexus*, edited by Robert Legvold, 107-140. Cambridge: MIT Press, 2003.

Hiro, Dilip. *Inside Central Asia: A Political and Cultural History of Uzbekistan, Turkmenistan, Kazakhstan, Kyrgyzstan, Tajikistan, Turkey, and Iran.* New York: Overlook Duckworth, Peter Mayer Publishers, Inc., 2009.

Hopkirk, Peter. *The Great Game: The Struggle for Empire in Central Asia.* New York: Kodansha International, 1992.

Ikenberry, G. John, ed. *America Unrivaled: the Future of the Balance of Power.* Ithaca: Cornell University Press, 2002.

Interstate Statistical Committee of the Commonwealth of Independent States. "About Commonwealth of Independent States." Interstate Statistical Committee of the Commonwealth of Independent States. http://www.cisstat.com/eng/cis.htm (accessed March 19, 2013).

Jonson, Lena. *Vladimir Putin and Central Asia: The Shaping of Russian Foreign Policy.* London: I. B. Tauris, 2004.

Joobani, Hossein Aghaie. "The Shanghai Cooperation Organization in Light of Organization Theory." e-International Relations. http://www.e-ir.info/2013/02/22/the-shanghai-cooperation-organization-in-light-of-organization-theory/ (accessed March 20, 2013).

Karrar, Hasan H. *The New Silk Road Diplomacy: China's Central Asian Foreign Policy Since the Cold War*. Vancouver: UBC Press, 2010.

Kucera, Joshua. "Central Asia: Washington Must Adapt to Diminished Role in Central Asia." Eurasianet.org. http://www.eurasianet.org/node/66253 (accessed March 20, 2013).

Legvold, Robert, ed. *Thinking Strategically: the Major Powers, Kazakhstan, and the Central Asian Nexus*. Cambridge: MIT Press, 2003.

Lizza, Ryan. "The Consequentialist: How the Arab Spring Remade Obama's Foreign Policy." The New Yorker. http://www.newyorker.com/reporting/2011/05/02/110502fa_fact_lizza (accessed November 18, 2012).

Martin, Kimberly *Disrupting the Balance: Russian Efforts to Control Kazakhstan's Oil*. New York: Columbia University - Barnard College, 2006. http://csis.org/files/media/csis/pubs/pm_0428.pdf (accessed March 18, 2013).

McDermott, Roger N. *The Kazakhstan-Russia Axis: Shaping CSTO Transformation*. Fort Leavenworth: Foreign Military Studies Office, 2011. http://fmso.leavenworth.army.mil/Collaboration/international/McDermott/CSTO_Transfo rmation-final.pdf (accessed March 20, 2013).

—. *Kazakhstan's 2011 Military Doctrine: Reassessing Regional and International Security*. Fort Leavenworth: Foreign Military Studies Office, 2011. http://fmso.leavenworth.army.mil/Collaboration/international/McDermott/CSTO_Transfo rmation-final.pdf (accessed August 8, 2012).

Mihalka, Michael D. "Not Much of a Game: Security Dynamics in Central Asia." *China and Eurasia Forum Quarterly* 5, no. 2 (May 2007): 21-39. http://www.silkroadstudies.org/new/docs/CEF/Quarterly/May_2007/Mihalka.pdf (accessed August 8, 2012).

Naumkin, Vitaly. "Russian Policy Toward Kazakhstan." In *Thinking Strategically: the Major Powers, Kazakhstan, and the Central Asian Nexus*, edited by Robert Legvold, 39-66. Cambridge: MIT Press, 2003.

Nichol, Jim. *The April 2010 Coup in Kyrgyzstan and Its Aftermath*. Washington: Congressional Research Service, 2010. http://www.dtic.mil/cgi-bin/GetTRDoc?Location=U2&doc=GetTRDoc.pdf&AD=ADA523588 (accessed March 20, 2013).

—. *Uzbekistan's Closure of the Airbase at Karshi-Khanabad: Context and Implications*. Washington: Congressional Research Service, 2005. http://digital.library.unt.edu/ark:/67531/metacrs7519/m1/1/high_res_d/RS22295_2005Oc t07.pdf (accessed March 20, 2013).

North Atlantic Treaty Organization. "NATO's Relations with Kazakhstan." North Atlantic Treaty Organization. http://www.nato.int/cps/en/natolive/topics_49598.htm (accessed September 27, 2012).

Organization of the Petroleum Exporting Countries. "Member Countries" Organization of the Petroleum Exporting Countries. http://www.opec.org/opec_web/en/about_us/25.htm (accessed March 18, 2013).

PLA Daily. "The 9 Joint Military Exercises under SCO Framework." PLA Daily of the Chinese People's Liberation Army. http://eng.chinamil.com.cn/special-reports/2012-06/12/content_4892903.htm (accessed March 18, 2013).

Scheineson, Andrew. "The Shanghai Cooperation Organization." Council on Foreign Relations. http://www.cfr.org/international-peace-and-security/shanghai-cooperation-organization/p10883 (accessed March 20, 2013).

Slantchev, Branislav L. "Introduction to International Relations, Lecture 3: The Rational Actor Model." Lecture, University of California, San Diego, San Diego, CA, April 19, 2005. http://slantchev.ucsd.edu/courses/ps12/03-rational-decision-making.pdf (accessed August 8, 2012).

Snyder, Jack. "One World, Rival Theories." Foreign Policy. http://www.foreignpolicy.com/articles/2004/11/01/one_world_rival_theories (accessed April 2, 2013).

Stein, Matthew. *Compendium of Central Asian Military and Security Activity.* Fort Leavenworth: Foreign Military Studies Office, 2012. http://fmso.leavenworth.army.mil/documents/Central-Asian-Military-Events.pdf (accessed March 20, 2013).

Sultanov, Bulat, and Leila Muzaparova. "Great Power Policies and Interests in Kazakhstan." In *Thinking Strategically: the Major Powers, Kazakhstan, and the Central Asian Nexus,* edited by Robert Legvold, 187-216. Cambridge: MIT Press, 2003.

Swanson, Michael J. "The New Great Game: A Phase Zero, Regional Engagement Strategy for Central Asia." Monograph, United States Army Command and General Staff College - School of Advanced Military Studies, 2007. In Defense Technical Information Center, http://www.dtic.mil/cgi-bin/GetTRDoc?AD=ADA479438 (accessed August 8, 2012).

Thucydides. *The Landmark Thucydides: A Comprehensive Guide to the Peloponnesian War.* Edited by Robert Strassler. New York: Free Press, 1998.

Tirpak, John A. "Project Sapphire" airforce-magazine.com. http://www.airforce-magazine.com/MagazineArchive/Pages/1995/August%201995/0895sapphire.aspx (accessed March 19, 2013).

U.S. Energy Information Administration. *Kazakhstan.* Washington: U.S. Energy Information Administration, 2012. http://www.eia.gov/countries/analysisbriefs/Kazakhstan/kazakhstan.pdf (accessed March 18, 2013).

United States Air Force. "Fact Sheets." Transit Center at Manas. http://www.manas.afcent.af.mil/library/factsheets/index.asp (accessed March 22, 2013).

United States Army. *Army Doctrine Reference Publication ADRP 5-0: The Operations Process.* Washington: Department of the Army, 2012.

——. *Field Manual FM 3-22: Army Support to Security Cooperation.* Washington: Department of the Army, 2013.

Van Evera, Stephen. *Guide to Methods for Students of Political Science.* Ithaca: Cornell University Press, 1997.

Verleger, Philip K. *Adjusting to Volatile Energy Prices.* Washington: Peterson Institute, 1994.

Walt, Stephen M. "International Relations: One World, Many Theories." *Foreign Policy* no. 110 (Spring 1998): 29-45. http://www.jstor.org/stable/10.2307/1149275 (accessed September 28, 2012).

——. "Keeping the World "Off-Balance": Self-Restraint and U.S. Foreign Policy." In *America Unrivaled: The Future of the Balance of Power*, edited by G. John Ikenberry, 121-254. Ithaca: Cornell University Press, 2002.

Waltz, Kenneth N. "Structural Realism after the Cold War." In *America Unrivaled: the Future of the Balance of Power*, edited by G. John Ikenberry, 29-67. Ithaca: Cornell University Press, 2002.

World Nuclear Association. "Uranium and Nuclear Power in Kazakhstan." World Nuclear Association. http://www.world-nuclear.org/info/inf89.html (accessed April 2, 2013).